CardMaker's

Hand-Lettering

WORKBOOK

CardMaker's Hand-Lettering Workbook

EDITOR Tanya Fox

CREATIVE DIRECTOR Brad Snow

PUBLISHING SERVICES DIRECTOR
Brenda Gallmeyer

ASSOCIATE EDITOR Brooke Smith

ASSISTANT ART DIRECTOR Nick Pierce

COPY SUPERVISOR Deborah Morgan

COPY EDITORS Emily Carter,
Rebecca Detwiler, Samantha Schneider

TECHNICAL EDITOR Corene Painter

PHOTOGRAPHY SUPERVISOR
Tammy Christian

PHOTO STYLISTS Tammy Liechty,
Tammy Steiner

PHOTOGRAPHY Matthew Owen

PRODUCTION ARTIST SUPERVISOR
Erin Brandt

GRAPHIC ARTIST Nicole Gage

PRODUCTION ASSISTANTS Marj Morgan,
Judy Neuenschwander

TECHNICAL ARTIST Debera Kuntz

ISBN: 978-1-59635-378-7
Printed in USA
1 2 3 4 5 6 7 8 9

CONTENTS

FOreWORD

In an age where cellphones, computers and other electronic devices have become the primary means of communication, sending and receiving hand-written notes and letters is sadly becoming a thing of the past. Recent news reports even suggest that penmanship and handwriting curriculums are being eliminated in some school systems. In our fast-paced society, few people have—or take—the time to sit and write letters.

Card makers and paper crafters are among the group of people who remain committed to sending greeting cards and creating memory pages that include the ultimate personal expression of a handwritten note or sentiment. A few penned lines convey the message that the creator of the piece wanted her creation to reflect a bit of herself and cared enough to share that with others. These carefully crafted pieces are held and treasured by those who receive them, the handwriting inside prompting fond recollections of the individual who sent it. In the same way, unfolding a letter from a great-grandmother has a way of bringing her close again.

Expert penmanship is achieved over time and with much practice, but it is an attainable goal. Nancy Burke and Marian Rodenhizer are two individuals who are passionate about hand lettering and love sharing their artful lettering with others.

Nancy believes that anyone who can write can become a lettering artist. Writing is something we learn at an early age, and with just a little practice, each and every one of the 26 letters of the alphabet can become so much more than letters—artwork in and of themselves. Using each of the basic letters as your starting point, and with just a little bit of creative effort, hand lettering can be a way to express thoughts through words in a beautiful way.

Marian, a professional calligrapher, has turned her passion for working with ink and paper into a full-time business of hand lettering invitations for brides and event planners across the country and around the world. She's expanded her business to include beautifully lettered, hand-bound books and journals as well.

Whether you're an advanced crafter or just venturing into the wonderful world of paper crafts, lovely hand-lettered cards, memory pages and journals are just a few pen strokes away. With easy-to-follow tutorials, eye-catching sample projects to inspire you and lots of room to practice, let *CardMaker's Hand-Lettering Workbook* open up the wonderful world of hand lettering.

HAND-LETTERING BASICS

By Nancy Burke

For the various lettering styles featured in this book, several tools were essential in achieving the end results. The tools listed below are "must haves" for any successful hand-lettering style.

Pencils

When setting out to create your own hand lettering on cards and other projects, your pencil will become the most important tool you own. Although it is best to begin with a No. 2 pencil, keep in mind that not all pencils are created equal! A good-quality graphite pencil for tracing is best and can be purchased at any art supply store. Lesser-quality pencils are more easily accessible, but be wary of these "dime-a-dozen" pencils. A good-quality pencil may cost a little more, but will be well worth it in the end. Be sure to keep any good-quality writing instruments separate from the rest of the family's pencils and tools. Protect your investment!

Another important thing to consider is how easy it is for the pencil lines to be erased. Many pencil manufacturers use additives in their pencil leads for more permanence so that they are less likely to smudge. This is great for keeping notes and making grocery lists, but is not ideal for the lettering artist. When you attempt to erase the lead from these pencils, it may be difficult to remove all visible pencil lines. Test out how easily a pencil can be erased as well as how it writes before using it on a project.

Erasers

Most high-quality pencils do not have an eraser attached to the end. So you will need to purchase a good eraser separately from your pencil. White erasers seem to work best and have no trouble erasing most pencil lines that are written with standard pressure. Long, white erasers that can be reloaded into a pen-style instrument are a good tool to have handy. When you wear down the eraser tip, simply advance the eraser in the cartridge. Other types of erasers that work well are small, white block erasers. Although after several uses, the corners can wear down, leaving you with an eraser "ball" that may not work for erasing small areas or tight corners.

Colored & Watercolor Pencils

Colored pencils are pencils that contain pigment rather than graphite. Colored pencils that contain water-soluble pigment are referred to as watercolor pencils or simply watercolors. Colored pencils are fun to experiment with and can create a variety of looks to any finished lettering style. Watercolor pencils can be used to lightly color in an area, and then use a paintbrush dipped in water or a water-filled pen to create further shading with a smooth, even appearance.

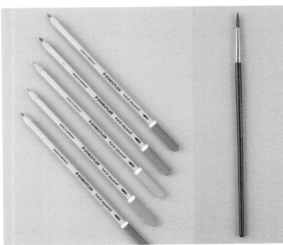

Pens & Markers

Pens and markers used for hand lettering come in all styles and colors, as well as many different tips, each one creating a different and unique look. Experimenting with these tools can be enjoyable and fun. Different tips include brush, chisel and monoline, as well as tips ranging from ultrafine/fine to bold/wide.

Fine and ultrafine tips are best for outlining and adding smaller decorative details.

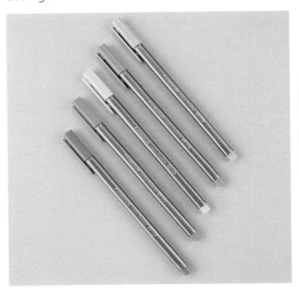

Fine to medium tips are used for basic lettering styles and are the standard size used in the completed alphabets throughout this book. Wide-tip, or bold-tip markers and pens can be used for drawing larger letters as well as filling in open spaces in many decorative lettering styles.

For most projects, high-quality, medium-weight cardstock in a light color is best. Because paper fibers can easily be broken down by moisture, use paper especially made for watercolor application when using watercolor pencils. Always test paper for fiber durability when using water soluble colored pencils and markers.

Papers

Just as writing instruments come in a wide variety of styles and colors, there are also limitless possibilities in the type of paper in which to apply your hand lettering. Graph paper is an excellent surface to practice on, as the grids and lines will help you keep letter lines straight and letters evenly spaced. Feel free to take a piece of tracing paper and copy over lettering samples provided in this book. This will help you with proportions and shape.

Lightbox

Another tool that can be useful in hand lettering is a lightbox. Although not an essential item, a lightbox makes it easier to trace letters as well as other decorative elements that may be more difficult to draw freehand. A lightbox works well when using thicker papers that are not as transparent as a thinner, standard-weight paper. A lightbox also eliminates the need to draw guidelines onto your finished lettering surface. ■

Lined paper is also a great surface to practice on; lined practice sheets have been included with this book. For finished projects and cards, the sky's the limit when it comes to paper that can be used. Just remember that heavier paper will hold up better, but may be difficult to see through while tracing.

BLOCK

This lettering style can either be drawn following a baseline, or completely free-form with letters slightly below or above the adjacent letter. Practice first by drawing on a baseline and then when comfortable, experiment with letter placement.

Project note: *This is a very basic block lettering style that can be decorated, shaded and embellished in so many fun and whimsical ways. Get creative and have fun!*

1. Using a pencil, lightly draw basic uppercase letters. Be sure to leave enough space between each letter for altering.

2. Using a larger-tip marker, outline each letter to widen them, being careful to make each letter roughly the same width.

3. Erase all pencil lines, leaving only the outline.

4. Using a fine-tip pen, outline the colored marker as shown below.

5. Using watercolor pencils, watercolors or regular colored pencils, shade in letter from top to bottom and light to dark.

Font created by Nancy Burke

A B D J

A B C D E

F G H I J

K L M N O P

Q R S T U

V W X Y Z

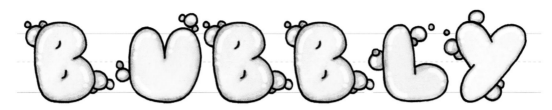

This lettering style can either be drawn following a baseline or completely free-form with letters slightly below or above the adjacent letter. Practice first by drawing on a baseline and then when comfortable, experiment with letter placement.

Project note: *This alphabet is a truly free-form alphabet and can be as fun and whimsical as you want to make it. There are no hard rules to this lettering style other than to make sure you do not get so carried away that the letters lose their readability. Just about anything that has a rounded edge, whether it be balloons, bubbles or even chocolate chip cookies, can be drawn using this style.*

1. Lightly draw basic uppercase letters. Be sure to leave enough space between each letter for altering.

2. Draw a wide, rounded outline around each letter, taking care that every part of the letter is round with no straight lines. You can create an overlapped look at this point by outlining each letter to appear to be "tucked" behind an adjacent letter.

3. Using a fine-tip pen or marker, trace over outline. Erase any visible pencil lines.

4. Color letters in with colored pencils, watercolors or markers. Shade and create further dimension by adding decorative elements, such as additional smaller bubbles and reflection marks.

Font created by Nancy Burke

casual

Using a pencil, lightly draw a base, middle and top guideline where you wish your sentiment or title to appear. Following these guidelines closely will ensure that all letters are the same height. Make sure that there is an even amount of space below, above and along each edge of your finished letter to accommodate adjustments made in each step.

Project note: *This lettering style looks best when done with a fine- to medium-tip pen. When drawn with an opaque pen or marker onto dark paper, a very dramatic look can be achieved. This lettering style is also quite elegant when done with a calligraphy pen or marker. Experiment with several types of pen and marker tips and colors to get a variety of looks. Ascenders and descenders are extended—double the height and depth.*

1. Keeping bottom edge of all letters touching your baseline, and tilting hand slightly to create a slanted, italic appearance to each letter, carefully draw out your sentiment or title in cursive using a pencil. Doing this in a slow and steady manner will ensure that all letters are slanted the same angle.

2. Trace over your original letters, making sure to exaggerate the ascenders and descenders, elongating serifs.

3. Trace over adjusted pencil lines with a fine- to medium-tip pen or marker. Allow adequate time for pen ink to dry completely and erase any visible pencil lines.

Font created by Marian Rodenhizer

A B C D

A B C D E F G H

I J K L M N O

P Q R S T U V

W X Y Z

This lettering style can either be drawn following a baseline (as in the steps below), or letters can be drawn free-form to appear to "bounce" (as in Bridal Shower Invitation card on page 46). If drawn free-form, you may wish to use a ruler simply to keep letters roughly the same height and width.

Project note: *This alphabet is one of the easiest ways to turn a basic lettering style into something truly decorative and unique. The sky's the limit when it comes to designs and objects that can be drawn at the ends of each letter line. Imagine pretty pink buttons for a sweet baby shower invitation or baseballs for a sports fan's birthday card.*

1. Lightly draw each letter in your sentiment or title, making sure enough space is left between each letter to add flowers or other decorative details to the ends of each letter line.

2. Draw small, decorative images and designs, such as hearts or flowers, at the ends of each letter line.

3. Using a fine-tip pen or marker, trace over lines. Color in decorative details with colored pencils, watercolors or markers. Erase any visible pencil lines.

4. You can further embellish each letter by drawing additional wavy lines over the straight letter lines.

Font created by Nancy Burke

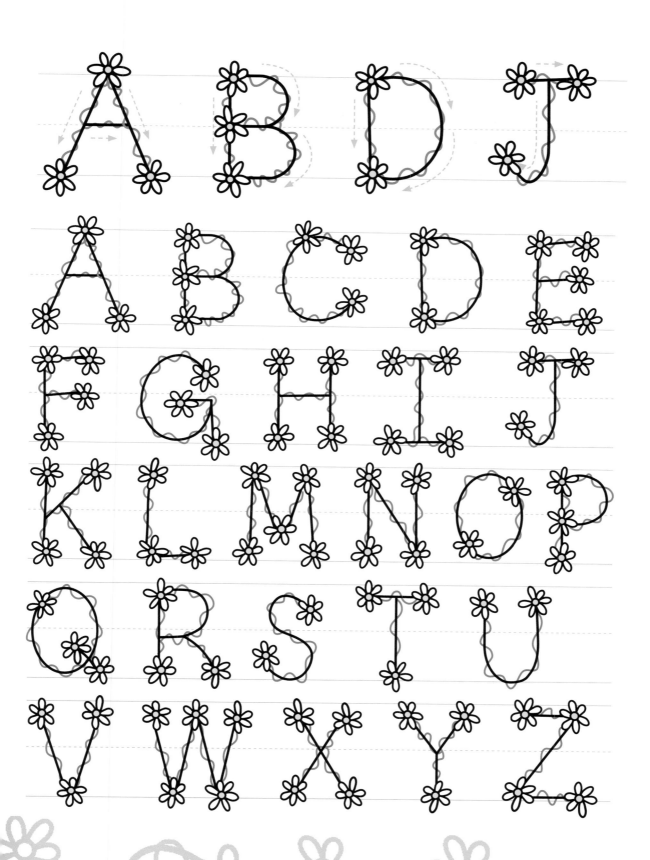

EVERYDAY

The Everyday Alphabet is another good example of a lettering style that can be practiced in order to build basic lettering skills. After drawing your guidelines lightly with a pencil, trace or draw directly onto the paper until you feel comfortable with the appearance of your letters.

Project note: *This lettering style looks best when following the base and top guidelines closely. This alphabet lends itself to a very natural combination of printed and cursive letters. Feel free to sometimes join the letters and other times let them stand alone. This alphabet looks best when a combination of upper and lower case is used. The use of a calligraphy pen can also make this lettering style quite elegant.*

Font created by Marian Rodenhizer

A B C D

A B C D E
F G H I g
K L M N O P
Q R S T U
V W X Y z

FANCY

Using a pencil, lightly draw a base, middle and top guideline where you wish your sentiment or title to appear. Following these guidelines will ensure that all letters are relatively the same in height.

Project note: *This lettering style can be kept simple or very decorative with extra flourishes. Try experimenting by adding additional curls to already curly letter lines as in the Fancy Monogram Card on page 48.*

1. Keeping bottom edge of all letters touching your baseline, and tilting hand slightly to create a slanted appearance to each letter, carefully draw out your sentiment or title in cursive using a pencil. Doing this in a slow and steady manner will ensure that all letters are slanted the same angle.

2. Using a pencil, embellish each letter by exaggerating serifs and curls at the ends of letter lines. Refer to finished alphabet for suggested adjustments.

3. Trace over letters with a fine- to medium-tip marker. Allow adequate time for pen ink to dry completely and erase any visible pencil lines.

Font created by Marian Rodenhizer

A B C D

A B C D E F G

H I J K L M

N O P Q R S T

U V W X Y Z

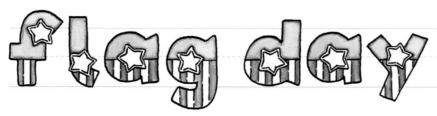

Draw your baseline where you would like the bottom of each letter to "sit." These letters will be rather wide when completed, so be sure to allow adequate spacing between each letter. Lightly draw a middle and top line to ensure letters are the same height as well.

Project note: *This alphabet can be one of the more difficult lettering styles to master. But with a little practice, it will easily become a favorite. Be sure to follow each step for all letters before moving onto the next step, rather than completing one letter at a time. This will ensure that letters are more uniform in their overall appearance.*

1. Using a pencil, lightly draw basic lowercase letters.

2. Draw an outline around each letter to widen them, being careful to make each roughly the same width. You may also make the bottom half of each letter slightly wider than the top half. This will give letters a slight "bell bottom" appearance as in the It's a Picnic card on page 49.

3. Erase original center pencil lines.

4. In the center of each letter, draw a small image or object. This could be a star, a flower or, as in the It's a Picnic card, a watermelon seed.

5. To further embellish letters, draw stripes on the bottom half of each letter and color in with colored pencils, watercolors or markers.

Font created by Nancy Burke

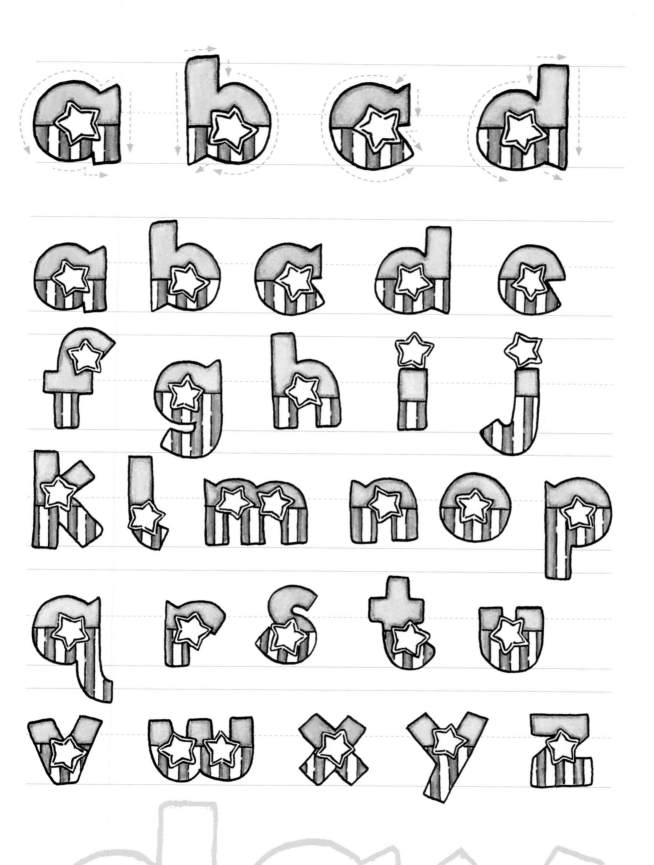

Using a pencil, draw your baseline where you would like the bottom of each letter to "sit." To keep letters the same height, you may also wish to draw a top guideline as well. Be sure to leave enough room at the beginning and end of your sentiment or title, as well as between each letter, to add decorative serifs.

Project note: *This alphabet is a variation of the very popular Art Deco lettering style. This is typically seen as an all-caps font and has better readability as such, but with a little practice, can be done in lowercase letters as well.*

1. Using a pencil, lightly draw basic letters, keeping them nearly as wide as they are tall.

2. Using a straightedge or ruler to keep lines straight, widen the left main vertical line of each letter.

3. Add serifs to the ends of each letter line. Serifs can either be straight, curly or a combination of both. Curly serifs can either be open swirls or closed circles. Refer to complete alphabet for serif style and placement.

4. Using a fine-tip pen or marker, trace over lines. Erase any visible pencil lines. Draw small decorative elements such as flowers or hearts. Or, start in the widened area of each letter and fill in letters with colored pencils, watercolors or markers.

Font created by Nancy Burke

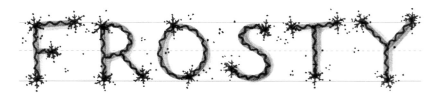

This lettering style can either follow a baseline, or be more free-form. Similar to the Daisy Alphabet, use a ruler to keep each individual letter roughly the same height and width and to keep letter lines straight.

Project note: *This is a simple, yet fun alphabet that can be used for just about anything by changing the snowflakes to simple dots. You can also make it very artistic and unique by adding almost any type of decorative element you can think of. Try mixing uppercase and lowercase letters for a more whimsical look.*

1. Lightly draw each letter in your sentiment or title, making sure enough space is left between each letter to add snowflakes or other decorative details to the ends of each letter line.

2. Erase any visible pencil lines, leaving small dots at the intersections and ends of each letter line as shown. These will serve as your guide in the next step.

3. Using a slightly wide and lighter-colored marker or colored pencil, reconnect points to re-form all letter lines.

4. Using a darker, fine-tip pen or marker, trace over letter lines in a wavy manner. You may wish to practice this on scratch paper until you feel comfortable and have a consistent wrist motion.

5. Draw small decorative images and designs, such as snowflakes, hearts or flowers, at the ends of each letter line and at dots.

Font created by Nancy Burke

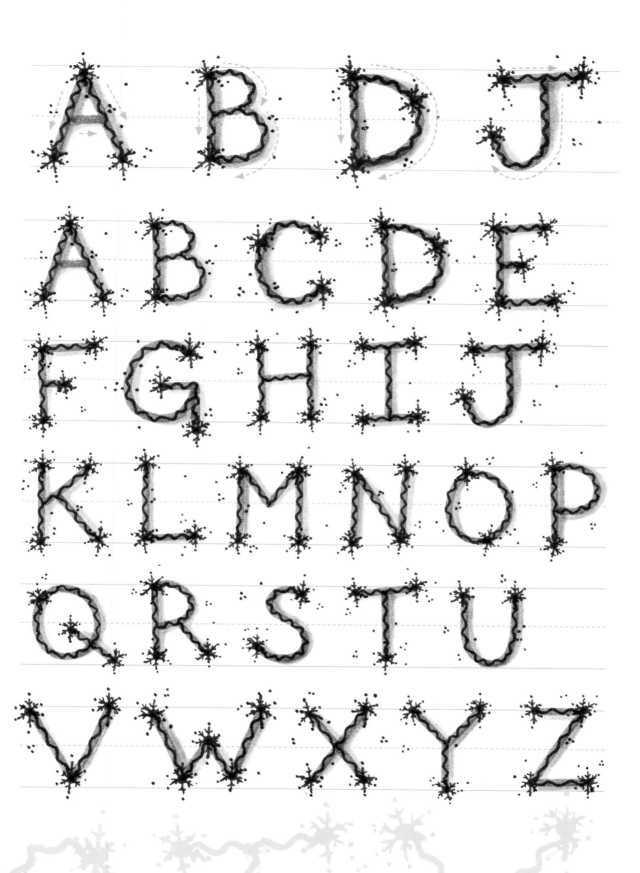

Due to the uniqueness of this lettering style, and the fact that it lends itself well to a "bouncing" appearance, it is best to begin by using a pencil to lightly draw boxes for each letter. Keep each box similar in shape and size to ensure the finished letters follow suit.

Project note: *This alphabet is lots of fun once you get the hang of it! The best part is filling it in with your own colorful elements and artwork. Try ladybugs for a fun summer party or big, bold blooms for that '70s "flower power" look.*

1. Lightly draw basic uppercase letters inside each box, leaving a little room around each letter for widening.

2. Widen each letter so that the bottom half is slightly wider than the top half. This will create "bell bottom" appearance to the letters.

3. Trace over outline with a fine-tip pen or marker and erase any visible pencil lines.

4. Create a dimensional shadow effect by creating a second, thin outline at the bottom and left side of each letter. Fill in letters with decorative elements, such as stripes, polka dots or other line art, using colored pencils, watercolors or markers.

Font created by Nancy Burke

Draw your baseline where you would like the bottom of each letter to "sit." Be sure to leave enough room at the beginning and end of your sentiment or word to add decorative serifs. You may also wish to draw a top guideline as well in order to keep letters the same height.

Project note: *This lettering style is very feminine, but can easily be adapted for more masculine projects. Replace the curly serifs with straight lines, and opt for a less feminine center element.*

1. Lightly draw basic letters, keeping them nearly as wide as they are tall.

2. Widen the left or right main vertical line of each letter.

3. Create a slight flare at the bottom and top of each widened area of each letter and add double curly serifs to the ends of letter lines.

4. Using a fine-tip pen or marker, trace over lines. Erase any visible pencil lines.

5. Lightly draw additional decorative elements such as bows, flowers or stars in the centers of flared areas. Finish by coloring letters with colored pencils, watercolors or markers.

Font created by Nancy Burke

ROMAN

Using a pencil, lightly draw a base and top guideline where you wish your sentiment or title to appear. Following these guidelines closely will ensure that all letters are the same height.

Project note: *At first glance, this lettering style may appear to be rather simple, but it can be quite difficult to master in its near perfect uniformity. Be careful to keep your proportions accurate. As with any lettering style, practice makes perfect! This lettering style also lends itself to unlimited variety by using extra pens and pencils to highlight and emphasize each letter.*

1. Keeping bottom edge of all letters touching your baseline and using a pencil, lightly draw each letter of your sentiment or title. Bowls of lowercase letters are slightly slanted. You may wish to draw each letter using a ruler or other straightedge.

2. Trace over pencil lines with a fine- to medium-tip pen or marker. Allow adequate time for pen ink to dry completely and erase any visible pencil lines.

3. Try bouncing letters for a fun and casual look. Keep the proportion and size of each letter consistent but raise or lower each letter from the baseline. Twist the letters slightly to give it more variation.

Font created by Marian Rodenhizer

A B D J

A B C D E

F G H I J

K L M N O P

Q R S T U

V W X Y Z

SUMMER

Using a pencil, lightly draw a base, middle and top guideline where you wish your sentiment or title to appear. Make sure that there is an even amount of space below, above and along each edge of your finished letter to accommodate adjustments made in each step below.

Project note: *This is a very easy lettering style to master with only a minimal amount of effort. A few practice strokes on a scratch piece of paper, and you will be using this versatile yet whimsical lettering style on all of your cards and projects. This alphabet lends itself to "bouncing" letters to give an overall fun and casual look.*

1. Keeping the bottom edge of all letters touching your baseline, and using a pencil, lightly draw each letter of your sentiment or title.

2. Since this lettering style is based on an oval shape, go back over the bowls (rounded areas) of each letter, slightly widening them to create a horizontal oval. Keep these ovals small and compact, while longer vertical lines, as well as ascenders and descenders can be exaggerated and lengthened.

3. Lightly draw very small serifs to the ends of each letter line. Refer to complete alphabet for placement of serifs.

4. Trace over entire letter with a fine- to medium-tip pen or marker. Allow adequate time for pen ink to dry completely and erase any visible pencil lines.

Font created by Marian Rodenhizer

A B D J

A B C D E

F G H I J

K L M N O P

Q R S T U

V W X Y Z

This alphabet can either be drawn following a baseline or completely free-form with letters slightly below or above the adjacent letter. Practice first by drawing on a baseline and then when comfortable, experiment with letter placement.

Project note: *This alphabet is best when drawn in all uppercase letters For better readability, this alphabet is best when drawn in all uppercase letters. Any object that is relatively straight can be drawn for this lettering style. Try drawing rulers or baseball bats for a truly one-of-a-kind look.*

1. Lightly draw basic uppercase letters. Be sure to leave enough space between each letter so that you have plenty of room to widen letter lines and add decorative details. For rounded letters, draw several shorter, connected straight lines in place of rounded lines.

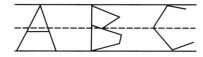

2. Slightly widen each letter line. Draw widened lines so that they overlap one another. Refer to completed alphabet for placement of overlapped areas. For boards, keep ends of widened lines straight, and for twigs, keep ends slightly curved.

3. Trace over lines with a fine-tip pen or marker. Erase original pencil lines.

4. Draw in details with a fine-tip pen or marker and color in letters with colored pencils, watercolors or markers.

Font created by Nancy Burke

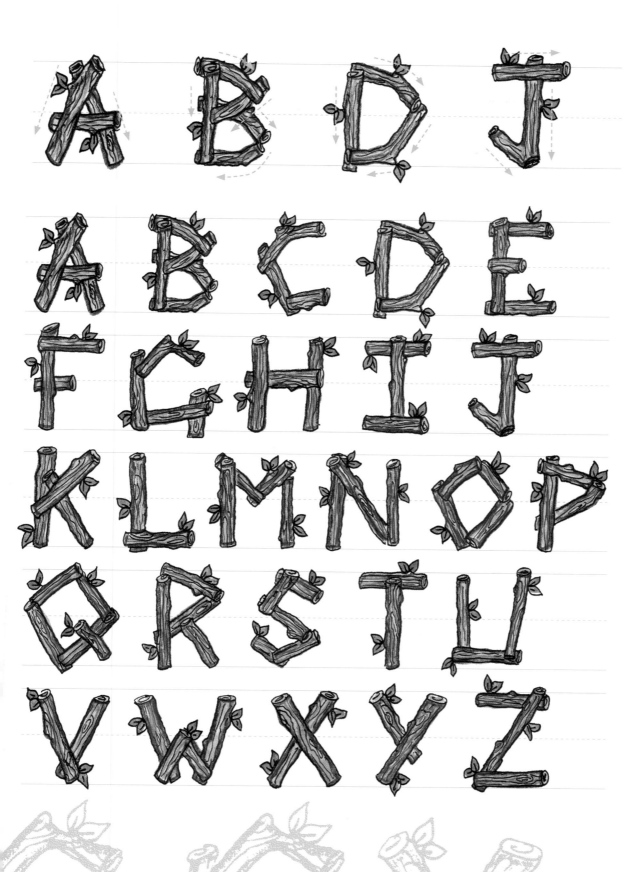

TYPEWRITER

Using a pencil, lightly draw a base, middle and top guideline where you wish your sentiment or title to appear. This lettering style looks best when using a medium-tip pen. Use a ruler to keep letters straight both vertically and horizontally, as there is no slant to this lettering style.

Project note: *This lettering style is boxy and bold, but different looks can be achieved by experimenting with different pen and marker points. For a look that truly makes a statement, try using a larger-tip pen. Always draw your letters in pencil first to ensure that spacing of letters is accurate.*

1. Keeping bottom edge of all letters touching your baseline, and using a pencil, lightly draw each letter of your sentiment or title.

2. Add short, straight serifs to the ends of all letter lines. Refer to completed alphabet for correct length and placement of serifs.

3. Trace over pencil lines with a medium-tip pen or marker. Allow adequate time for pen ink to dry completely and erase any visible pencil lines.

ABC

Font created by Marian Rodenhizer

A B D J

ABCDE

FGHIJ

KLMNOP

QRSTU

VWXYZ

vacation

Using a pencil, lightly draw a base, middle and top guideline where you wish your sentiment or title to appear. Following these guidelines will ensure that all letters are the same in height. This lettering style looks best when done in all lowercase letters.

Project note: *This lettering style is very loose and open to several interpretations. This alphabet is based on an oval shape even for letters such as r, h, t. The "o" is a sideways oval. Keep it at the the top of the ascender line. Dress up letters even further by adding curly or straight serifs to the ends of letter lines for a more expressive look.*

1. Using a pencil, lightly draw each letter of your sentiment or title.

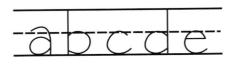

2. Go back over the pencil lines of each letter, slightly curving straight lines and adding exaggerating curls and descenders to each letter. Refer to complete alphabet for suggested adjustments.

3. Trace over adjusted pencil lines with a fine- to medium-tip pen or marker. Allow adequate time for pen ink to dry completely and erase any visible pencil lines.

Font created by Marian Rodenhizer

a b d j

a b c d e f g h

i j k l m n o

p q r s t u

v w x y z

WEEKEND

Using a pencil, lightly draw a base and top guideline where you wish your sentiment or title to appear. This lettering style looks best when done in all uppercase letters.

Project note: *This whimsical lettering style lends itself well to many different projects. For a bolder look, use a wide-tip marker or pen in a fun, vibrant color. This alphabet is based on the oval shape also—think tall and narrow.*

Although this lettering style looks best when done in all uppercase letters, familiarizing yourself with the overall alphabet will allow you to experiment with writing lowercase as well.

1. Using a pencil, lightly draw each letter of your sentiment or title.

2. Go back over the pencil lines of each letter, slightly tilting straight lines and exaggerating rounded areas of each letter. Descenders may also be lengthened and exaggerated in this step.

3. Lightly draw very small serifs onto the ends of a few letter lines. Refer to complete alphabet for placement of serifs.

4. Trace over adjusted pencil lines with a fine- to medium-tip pen or marker. Allow adequate time for pen ink to dry completely and erase any visible pencil lines.

Font created by Marian Rodenhizer

A B D J

A B C D E F

G H I J K K L

M N O P Q

R R S T U V

W X Y Y Z

PROJECT GALLERY

BLOCK

Lettering and designs by Nancy Burke

Time for Cake

Sources: *Cardstock from Die Cuts With A View; printed papers from BasicGrey, Webster's Pages and Bella BLVD; fine-tip pen from Faber-Castell USA Inc.; dual-tip markers from Tombow; watercolor pencils from General Pencil Company Inc.; alphabet stickers from Kaisercraft; scallop-edge scissors from Plaid Enterprises Inc.*

Happy Spring

Sources: *Cardstock from Die Cuts With A View and Bazzill Basics Paper Inc.; printed papers from Webster's Pages and October Afternoon; alphabet stickers from Making Memories; fine-tip pen from Faber-Castell USA Inc.; dual-tip markers from Tombow; watercolor pencils from General Pencil Company Inc.; pink stickpin from Maya Road; self-adhesive rhinestones from Kaisercraft.*

BUBBLY

Lettering and designs by Nancy Burke

Let's Have a Party!
Sources: *Cardstock from Die Cuts With A View; printed papers from Graphic 45 and Cosmo Cricket; alphabet stickers from Kaisercraft; fine-tip pen and metallic marker from Faber-Castell USA Inc.; watercolor pencils from General Pencil Company Inc.*

Sweet Baby Boy Card
Sources: *Cardstock from Die Cuts With A View and Jillibean Soup; printed paper from My Mind's Eye; alphabet stickers from Kaisercraft; "boy" sticker from Making Memories; fine-tip pen and colored pencils from Faber-Castell USA Inc.; circle and scalloped circle punches from Marvy Uchida.*

CASUAL

Lettering by Marian Rodenhizer
Designs by Nancy Burke

Baby

Sources: Cardstock and glitter printed paper from Die Cuts With A View; remaining printed papers from The Girls' Paperie; distress ink pad and gel pen from Ranger Industries Inc.; paper flowers and rhinestone charm from Prima Marketing Inc.; self-adhesive pearl from Kaisercraft; border punches from Martha Stewart Crafts; corner rounder from Marvy Uchida.

Happy Valentine's Day

Sources: Cardstock and glitter printed paper from Die Cuts With A View; printed papers and flowers from Prima Marketing Inc.; gel pen from Ranger Industries Inc.; Apron Lace Border punch from Fiskars; scallop-edge scissors from Plaid Enterprises Inc.

DAISY

Lettering and designs by Nancy Burke

Bridal Shower Invitation

Sources: *Cardstock from Die Cuts With A View; printed papers from The Girls' Paperie and Die Cuts With A View; distress ink pad from Ranger Industries Inc.; fine-tip pen from Faber-Castell USA Inc.; self-adhesive pearls from Kaisercraft; flowers from Webster's Pages; Doily Lace Edge Punch from Martha Stewart Crafts; scallop-edge scissors from Fiskars.*

Be Mine

Sources: *Cardstock from Die Cuts With A View; printed paper from Echo Park Paper Co.; fine-tip pen from Faber-Castell USA Inc.; Copic® marker from Imagination International Inc.; dual-tip marker from Tombow; self-adhesive rhinestones from Prima Marketing Inc.; wooden die-cut flourish from The Dusty Attic; corner rounder from Marvy Uchida; scallop-edge scissors from Plaid Enterprises Inc.*

EVERYDAY

Lettering by Marian Rodenhizer
Designs by Nancy Burke

Birthday Wishes

Sources: *Cardstock from Die Cuts With A View; journaling card from Webster's Pages; printed paper from Prima Marketing Inc.; Gabrielle Chipboard stickers from Bo-Bunny Press; distress ink pad from Ranger Industries Inc.; self-adhesive rhinestones from Kaisercraft.*

Happy Anniversary

Sources: *Cardstock and printed cardstock from Die Cuts With A View; printed paper, heart lock charm, key charm and paper flower embellishments from Prima Marketing Inc.; fine-tip pen from Faber-Castell USA Inc.; scallop-edge scissors from Plaid Enterprises Inc.*

FANCY

Lettering by Marian Rodenhizer
Designs by Nancy Burke

New Baby Boy
Sources: *Cardstock from Die Cuts With A View; printed papers from Bella BLVD and The Girls' Paperie; fine-tip pen from Faber-Castell USA Inc.; dual-tip markers from Tombow; wooden die cuts from The Dusty Attic.*

Thinking of You
Sources: *Cardstock from Die Cuts With A View and Bazzill Basics Paper Inc.; printed papers from Graphic 45; fine-tip pen from Faber-Castell USA Inc.; dual-tip markers from Tombow; flower embellishments from Prima Marketing Inc.; pearl brad from Making Memories; Tattered Florals die (#656640) from Sizzix.*

Fancy Monogram Card
Sources: *Cardstock from Die Cuts With A View; printed papers and cutouts from Bo-Bunny Press; distress ink pad from Ranger Industries Inc.; crocheted flower from Prima Marketing Inc.; paper doily from Martha Stewart Crafts; self-adhesive light blue pearls from Kaisercraft; wave-edge scissors from Provo Craft.*

flag day

Lettering and designs by
Nancy Burke

You Are My Hero

Sources: Cardstock from Die Cuts With A View; printed papers from The Girls' Paperie and My Mind's Eye; fine-tip pen from Faber-Castell USA Inc.; watercolor pencils from General Pencil Company Inc.; star punch from Plaid Enterprises Inc.

It's a Picnic

Sources: White cardstock from Die Cuts With A View; kraft cardstock and printed papers from Jillibean Soup; distress ink pad from Ranger Industries Inc.; fine-tip pen from Faber-Castell USA Inc.; Copic® markers from Imagination International Inc.; paper-flower embellishment from Prima Marketing Inc.; crochet trim from The Girls' Paperie.

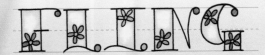

Lettering and designs by Nancy Burke

Happy Easter

Sources: *Cardstock from Die Cuts With A View and Jillibean Soup; printed papers from Pink Paislee; Easter Tweets Digi Stamps and doily digital die cut from MyGrafico; fine-tip pen and colored pencils from Faber-Castell USA Inc.; twine from Pink Paislee; flower embellishment from Prima Marketing Inc.; large scallop and small flower from Marvy Uchida; border punch from EK Success.*

For You

Sources: *Cardstock from Die Cuts With A View; printed papers from American Crafts Inc. and Anna Griffin Inc.; alphabet stickers and self-adhesive rhinestones from Kaisercraft; fine-tip pen from Faber-Castell USA Inc.; watercolor pencils from General Pencil Company Inc.; scallop-edge punch from Fiskars; Swiss Cheese Large Edger Punch From EK Success.*

Fling Monogram Card

Sources: *Printed papers from My Mind's Eye and Pink Paislee; chipboard frame and glitter spray from Tattered Angels; fine-tip pen from Faber-Castell USA Inc.; rose embellishment from Prima Marketing Inc.; decorative buttons from Webster's Pages; Apron Lace border punch from Fiskars.*

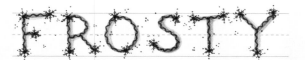

FROSTY

Lettering and designs by Nancy Burke

Winter Wishes
Sources: *Cardstock from Die Cuts With A View; printed paper from Best Creation Inc.; distress ink pad and gel pen from Ranger Industries Inc.; fine-tip pen from Faber-Castell USA Inc.; dual-tip marker from Tombow; snowflake charm from Darice Inc.; large scallop-circle punch from Marvy Uchida.*

Joy
Sources: *Cardstock from Die Cuts With A View; printed paper from The Girls' Paperie and BasicGrey; distress ink pad and gel pen from Ranger Industries Inc.; fine-tip pen from Faber-Castell USA Inc.; dual-tip marker from Tombow; button embellishments from The Girls' Paperie; scallop-edge scissors from Fiskars.*

FUNKY

Lettering and designs by Nancy Burke

Dude It's Your Birthday!
Sources: *Cardstock from Die Cuts With A View; printed paper and die cuts from Bella BLVD; fine-tip pen and metallic marker from Faber-Castell USA Inc.*

Fiesta Card
Sources: *Cardstock from Die Cuts With A View and Jillibean Soup; printed papers, die cut and crocheted trim from My Mind's Eye; distress ink pad from Ranger Industries Inc.; fine-tip pen from Faber-Castell USA Inc.; watercolor pencils from General Pencil Company Inc.; flower embellishment from Prima Marketing Inc.*

PRINCESS

Lettering and designs by Nancy Burke

Mandy Card

Sources: *Cardstock from Die Cuts With A View; printed papers from The Girls' Paperie and Bo-Bunny Press; dual-tip markers from Tombow; watercolor pencils from General Pencil Company Inc.; pink velvet scallop trim from Maya Road; crochet and plastic flower embellishments from Prima Marketing Inc.; decorative button from Webster's Pages; corner rounder and scallop-circle punch from Marvy Uchida.*

Princess Monogram Card

Sources: *Cardstock from Die Cuts With A View; printed papers, flower embellishments and crochet doily from Prima Marketing Inc.; distress ink pad from Ranger Industries Inc.; fine-tip pen and colored pencils from Faber-Castell USA Inc.; dual-tip marker from Tombow; decorative button from The Girls' Paperie; Doily Lace Edge Punch from Martha Stewart Crafts.*

ROMAN

Lettering by Marian Rodenhizer
Designs by Nancy Burke

Roman Gift Bag

Sources: *Cardstock from Die Cuts With A View, Bazzill Basics Paper Inc., The Girls' Paperie, Echo Park Paper Co. and Best Creation Inc.; paper doily and Hydrangea Punch from Martha Stewart Crafts; black flourish sticker from Stampendous! Inc.; dye ink pad from Ranger Industries Inc.; fine-tip pen from Faber-Castell USA Inc.; dual-tip marker from EK Success; white flower trim from Webster's Pages; large scallop-circle punch from Marvy Uchida; small scallop-circle punch from Fiskars; scallop-edge scissors from Plaid Enterprises Inc.*

Happy Birthday Card

Sources: *Cardstock from Die Cuts With A View; printed paper, stickers and green twine from Jillibean Soup; medium-tip marker from EK Success; gel pen from Ranger Industries Inc.*

SUMMER

Lettering by Marian Rodenhizer
Designs by Nancy Burke

Thank You Card
Sources: Cardstock from Die Cuts With A View; printed papers from Lily Bee Design, Pink Paislee and My Mind's Eye; fine-tip pen from Faber-Castell USA Inc.; dual-tip marker from Tombow; pearl button from Jenni Bowlin Studio; medium scallop-circle punch from Fiskars; small scallop-circle punch from Marvy Uchida.

Madeline Card
Sources: Cardstock from Die Cuts With A View and Bazzill Basics Paper Inc.; printed paper from Webster's Pages; fine-tip pen and colored pencils from Faber-Castell USA Inc.; scallop-edge scissors from Fiskars.

TWIGGY

Lettering and designs by Nancy Burke

Dad Card
Sources: *Cardstock from Die Cuts With A View and Jillibean Soup; printed papers from Little Yellow Bicycle and Crate Paper Inc.; wooden die cuts from The Dusty Attic; fine-tip pen from Faber-Castell USA Inc.; watercolor pencils from General Pencil Company Inc.; corner rounder from Marvy Uchida.*

Home Tweet Home
Sources: *Cardstock from Die Cuts With A View; printed papers from Webster's Pages, Bo-Bunny Press and BasicGrey; die-cut border sticker from Crate Paper Inc.; alphabet stickers from Kaisercraft; die cuts from The Dusty Attic; fine-tip pen from Faber-Castell USA Inc.; gel pen from Ranger Industries Inc.; watercolor pencils from General Pencil Company Inc.; Double Scallop-edge Punch from Martha Stewart Crafts.*

TYPEWRITER

Lettering by Marian Rodenhizer
Designs by Nancy Burke

Typewriter Gift Bag
Sources: *Cardstock from Die Cuts With A View; printed paper from American Crafts Inc.; fine-tip and medium-tip pens from Faber-Castell USA Inc.; corrugated button and green twine from Jillibean Soup; red and blue twine from Webster's Pages; wave-edge scissors from Provo Craft.*

Best Dad Card
Sources: *Cardstock from Die Cuts With A View; printed paper from Bella BLVD; distress ink pads from Ranger Industries Inc.; marker from EK Success; wave-edge scissors from Provo Craft.*

Typewriter Monogram Card
Sources: *Cardstock from Die Cuts With A View; printed paper from Echo Park Paper Co.; dual-tip pen from EK Success; yellow ruler-printed twill ribbon from Creative Impressions Inc.*

vacation

Lettering by Marian Rodenhizer
Designs by Nancy Burke

Be Merry Ornament
Sources: *Cardstock from Die Cuts With A View and Bazzill Basics Paper Inc.; blue glitter cardstock and printed paper from Best Creation Inc.; chipboard snowflake and red paint from Delta Creative Inc./ Rubber Stampede; fine-tip pen from Faber-Castell USA Inc.; dual-tip marker from Tombow; scallop-circle punch from Fiskars.*

Happy Christmas
Sources: *Cardstock from Jillibean Soup, American Crafts Inc. and Die Cuts With A View; printed papers from Bella BLVD and The Girls' Paperie; snowflake die cuts, lettering stickers and metal tag from The Girls' Paperie; fine-tip pen from Faber-Castell USA Inc.; ornament charm from Darice Inc.; fabric brad from BasicGrey; scallop-circle punch from Marvy Uchida.*

WEEKEND

Lettering by Marian Rodenhizer
Designs by Nancy Burke

Weekend Monogram Card
Sources: *Cardstock from Die Cuts With A View; printed papers, chipboard buttons and colored twine from Webster's Pages; fine-tip pen and metallic marker from Faber-Castell USA Inc.; dual-tip marker from EK Success; Apron Lace Border Punch from Fiskars.*

Invitation
Sources: *Cardstock from Die Cuts With A View and Bazzill Basics Paper Inc.; printed papers from Bella BLVD; fine-tip pen from Faber-Castell USA Inc.; self-adhesive rhinestones from Kaisercraft; plastic flower from Prima Marketing Inc.; Threading Water Border Punch from Fiskars; corner rounder from Marvy Uchida.*

PRACTICE

Copy this page as often as you need to for lettering practice.

PRACTICE

Copy this page as often as you need to for lettering practice.

We'd like to extend a special thank you to the following manufacturers for generously providing the products used to create the gallery projects.

American Crafts Inc.
(801) 226-0747
www.americancrafts.com

Anna Griffin Inc.
(888) 817-8170
www.annagriffin.com

BasicGrey
(801) 544-1116
www.basicgrey.com

Bazzill Basics Paper Inc.
(800) 560-1610
www.bazzillbasics.com

Bella BLVD
(414) 259-1800
www.bellablvd.net

Best Creation Inc.
www.bestcreation.us

Bo-Bunny Press
(801) 771-4010
www.bobunny.com

Cosmo Cricket
(800) 852-8810
www.cosmocricket.com

Crate Paper Inc.
(801) 798-8996
www.cratepaper.com

Creative Impressions Inc.
(719) 596-4860
www.creativeimpressions.com

Darice Inc.
(866) 432-7423
www.darice.com

Delta Creative Inc./Rubber Stampede
(800) 423-4135
www.deltacreative.com

Die Cuts With A View
(801) 224-6766
www.diecutswithaview.com

The Dusty Attic
www.dustyattic.ning.com

Echo Park Paper Co.
(800) 701-1115
www.echoparkpaper.com

EK Success
www.eksuccess.com

Faber-Castell USA Inc.
(800) 311-8684
www.designmemorycraft.com

Fiskars
(866) 348-5661
www.fiskarscrafts.com

General Pencil Company Inc.
(800) 537-0734
www.generalpencil.com

The Girls' Paperie
(904) 482-0091
www.thegirlspaperie.com

Graphic 45
(866) 573-4806
www.g45papers.com

Imagination International Inc.
(541) 684-0013
www.copicmarker.com

Jenni Bowlin Studio
www.jbsmercantile.com

Jillibean Soup
(888) 212-1177
www.jillibean-soup.com

Kaisercraft
(888) 684-7147
www.kaisercraft.net

Lily Bee Design
(801) 820-6845
www.lilybeedesign.com

Little Yellow Bicycle
(860) 286-0244
www.mylyb.com

Making Memories
(801) 294-0430
www.makingmemories.com

Martha Stewart Crafts
www.marthastewartcrafts.com

Marvy Uchida
(800) 541-5877
www.marvy.com

Maya Road
(877) 427-7764
www.mayaroad.com

MyGrafico
www.mygrafico.com

My Mind's Eye
(800) 665-5116
www.mymindseye.com

October Afternoon
(866) 513-5553
www.octoberafternoon.com

Pink Paislee
(800) 883-8259
www.pinkpaislee.com

Plaid Enterprises Inc.
(800) 842-4197
www.plaidonline.com

Prima Marketing Inc.
(909) 627-5532
www.primamarketinginc.com

Provo Craft
(800) 937-7686
www.provocraft.com

Ranger Industries Inc.
(732) 389-3535
www.rangerink.com

Sizzix
(877) 355-4766
www.sizzix.com

Stampendous! Inc.
(800) 869-0474
www.stampendous.com

Tattered Angels
(970) 622-9444
www.mytatteredangels.com

Tombow
www.tombowusa.com

Webster's Pages
(800) 543-6104
www.websterspages.com

The Buyer's Guide listings are provided as a service to our readers and should not be considered an endorsement from this publication.